25.99

D1116482

ANIMALS ON THE BRINK

Florida Manatees

J. D. Taylor

MEDIA ENHANCED BOOKS

AV²
BY WEIGL™

ADDED VALUE · AUDIO VISUAL

www.av2books.com

AV² provides enriched content that supplements and complements this book. Weigl's AV² books strive to create inspired learning and engage young minds in a total learning experience.

Your AV² Media Enhanced books come alive with...

Audio
Listen to sections of the book read aloud.

Key Words
Study vocabulary, and complete a matching word activity.

Video
Watch informative video clips.

Quizzes
Test your knowledge.

Embedded Weblinks
Gain additional information for research.

Slide Show
View images and captions, and prepare a presentation.

Try This!
Complete activities and hands-on experiments.

... and much, much more!

Go to **www.av2books.com**, and enter this book's unique code.

BOOK CODE

D978284

AV² by Weigl brings you media enhanced books that support active learning.

Published by AV² by Weigl
350 5th Avenue, 59th Floor
New York, NY 10118
Websites: www.av2books.com   www.weigl.com

Copyright ©2015 AV² by Weigl
All rights reserved. No part of this publication may be reproduced, stored in a retrieval system, or transmitted in any form or by any means, electronic, mechanical, photocopying, recording, or otherwise, without the prior written permission of the publisher.

Library of Congress Control Number: 2013953037

ISBN 978-1-4896-0560-3 (hardcover)
ISBN 978-1-4896-0561-0 (softcover)
ISBN 978-1-4896-0562-7 (single-user eBook)
ISBN 978-1-4896-0563-4 (multi-user eBook)

Printed in the United States of America in North Mankato, Minnesota
1 2 3 4 5 6 7 8 9   17 16 15 14 13

122013
WEP301113

Project Coordinator Aaron Carr
Design Mandy Christiansen

Every reasonable effort has been made to trace ownership and to obtain permission to reprint copyright material. The publishers would be pleased to have any errors or omissions brought to their attention so that they may be corrected in subsequent printings.

Photo Credits
Weigl acknowledges Getty Images as its primary photo supplier for this title.

Contents

Take a Stand

Debate • Research

The Florida Manatee

In the warm waters off the coast of Florida lives a fascinating animal called the manatee. This quiet, gentle animal has been mistaken for many other creatures, including a walrus. A manatee looks like a walrus in some ways. However, the walrus and the manatee are not closely related animals. In fact, the manatee is actually a closer relative of the elephant.

In this book, you will discover the world of the Florida manatee. Find out how long this animal can stay underwater. Learn why the manatee cannot drink salt water. Turn the page to enter the watery world of the Florida manatee.

American Indians in Florida used to call manatees "big beavers" because of their large, flat tails. This tail helps the Florida manatee travel great distances.

Manatees may resemble many other sea creatures, but they are not directly related to whales, seals, sea lions, or dolphins.

How to Take a Stand on an Issue

Research is important to the study of any scientific field. When scientists choose a subject to study, they must conduct research to ensure they have a thorough understanding of the topic. They ask questions about the subject and then search for answers. Sometimes, however, there is no clear answer to a question. In these cases, scientists must use the information they have to form a hypothesis, or theory. They must take a stand on one side of an issue or the other. Follow the process below for each Take a Stand section in this book to determine where you stand on these issues.

1. **What is the Issue?**
   a. Determine a research subject, and form a general question about the subject.

2. **Form a Hypothesis**
   a. Search at the library and online for sources of information on the subject.
   b. Conduct basic research on the subject to narrow down the general question.
   c. Form a hypothesis on the subject based on research to this point.
   d. Make predictions based on the hypothesis. What are the expected results?

3. **Research the Issue**
   a. Conduct extensive research using a variety of sources, including books, scientific journals, and reliable websites.
   b. Collect data on the issue and take notes on all information gathered from research.
   c. Draw conclusions based on the information collected.

4. **Conclusion**
   a. Explain the research findings.
   b. Was the hypothesis proved or disproved?

Keys to
Manatees

A manatee's inner earbones have growth layers, like tree rings, for each year of the animal's life.

The area around a manatee's mouth is covered with short, stiff whiskers called vibrissae. The vibrissae are very sensitive to touch and help the manatee identify food and other objects.

Features

Manatees are **mammals**. They have features that all mammals, including humans, share. Manatees have hair, which is scattered over their bodies. Mothers nurse their young with milk produced in their **mammary glands**.

Manatees are warm blooded. This means they can keep their body temperature about the same even though the temperature around them gets warmer or colder. Manatees breathe air, and they give birth to live young. Manatees are specially adapted to life in the water. They lack a defined neck. Their bodies have a blimp-like shape that helps the manatee glide smoothly through water.

A manatee uses its tail and flippers to move. Movement is powered by the pumping of the manatee's large, round tail. The tail moves the manatee forward and can also slow movement. All it takes is a slight angling of the tail to change the rate of movement. The flippers are used to steer the manatee in the direction it wants to go. The flippers also maneuver the manatee along the bottom of the water. The manatee looks like it is walking, but it is actually using its flippers to pull itself forward. The flippers are flexible and are also used to grasp food and other items. These features, along with several others, provide this large animal with an ideal body for its **aquatic** life.

When full-grown, Florida manatees reach an average length of between 10 and 12 feet (3 and 3.5 meters). The largest Florida manatee recorded was 13.5 feet (4.1 m). Females grow to be larger than males. An average Florida manatee weighs about 1,100 pounds (500 kilograms). The heaviest manatee ever recorded weighed 3,500 pounds (1,600 kg).

Manatees are capable of having long lives. A Florida manatee can live 60 years or more. One captive manatee reached 65 years of age.

Classification

There are three **species** of manatee. They are the West Indian manatee, the Amazonian manatee, and the West African manatee. Of these, the West Indian manatee is the largest. The Florida manatee is a subspecies, or type, of West Indian manatee. The three species belong to the **order** of animals called Sirenia. All Sirenians share common features, including a tube-shaped body, short flippers, a flattened tail, and an aquatic lifestyle. All Sirenians are plant-eaters.

The order Sirenia is divided into two families. Manatees belong to the family Trichechidae. The other family, Dugongidae, contains the dugongs, which are animals that closely resemble the manatee. The manatee shares a common ancestor with the elephant and a small, gopher-sized mammal called the hyrax.

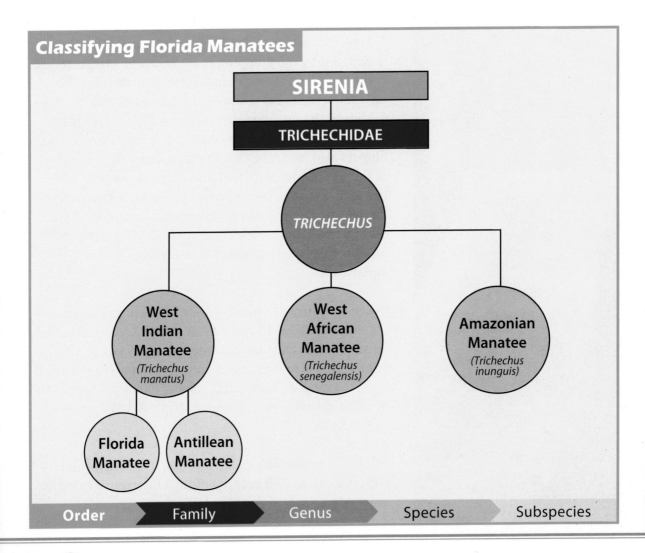

Classifying Florida Manatees

SIRENIA

TRICHECHIDAE

TRICHECHUS

West Indian Manatee (*Trichechus manatus*)

West African Manatee (*Trichechus senegalensis*)

Amazonian Manatee (*Trichechus inunguis*)

Florida Manatee

Antillean Manatee

Order → Family → Genus → Species → Subspecies

The Florida manatee is one of two subspecies of the West Indian manatee. Its scientific name, in Latin, is *Trichechus manatus latirostris*.

The Antillean manatee, or *Trichechus manatus manatus*, is a West Indian manatee subspecies. It lives in coastal waters and river systems of eastern Mexico, Central America, northern South America, and the Caribbean.

The Amazonian manatee species is found in the Amazon River basin.

Special Adaptations

Manatees need to breathe air in order to survive. They must go to the water's surface when they need to breathe. Manatees breathe only through their nostrils. This allows them to feed underwater without drowning. Florida manatees have many special features that help them live in the water.

Nostrils

A manatee's nostrils are located on the top of its snout. This allows the animal to poke only its nostrils out of the water and keep the rest of its body submerged. After the manatee has taken a breath, its nostrils close tightly with the help of valvelike flaps of skin, and the animal goes completely underwater again.

Mouth

A manatee's upper lip is **prehensile**. Divided into two sections, the upper lip is able to wrap around leaves and other plant parts, so that they can be pulled into the manatee's mouth.

Bones

Manatees can remain underwater with very little effort because of their heavy bones. The bones act like a diver's weight belt, which helps the diver stay underwater without sinking to the bottom.

Teeth

Manatees eat plants full of a hard, glassy mineral called silica. These very hard plants wear out manatee teeth. Manatees have "marching molars." This means that as the teeth wear down, they move forward in the mouth until they fall out. At the same time, new teeth are growing in the back of the mouth. A manatee has between 24 and 32 molars that are constantly being replaced over its lifetime.

Skin

The Florida manatee's rough skin can be up to 2 inches (5 centimeters) thick. Skin colors range from brown to gray. Sometimes, the skin has a greenish appearance, due to **algae** that grow on the manatee's back. Much like a snake, however, a manatee sheds its skin often. This helps get rid of the algae growth. Beneath the manatee's skin is a thin layer of blubber, or fat, that is normally less than 1 inch (2.5 cm) thick. The blubber helps the manatee stay warm and survive brief periods when the water temperature gets low.

Lungs

A manatee has very large lungs, which are used to store air and to control its **buoyancy**. If a manatee wants to go deep in the water, it contracts, or squeezes, its lungs. The squeezed air in the lungs takes up less space and increases the **density** of the manatee. This allows the animal to sink deeper. When the manatee wants to rise to the surface, it expands its lung muscles. This allows the air to spread out, and the animal floats upward.

Keys to
Manatees

Manatee species vary in size
but are similar in shape.

Like whales, dolphins, seals, and sea otters, manatees usually form groups
to find food or mates or to avoid animals that hunt them. However, the
only permanent manatee pairings in nature are a mother and her calf.

Groups

For the most part, the Florida manatee is a solitary animal. This means that it tends to have little contact with other members of its species. Manatees, therefore, have less need than other types of animals to develop complex social systems. This is not to say that manatees avoid contact with one another. Manatees come together for mating, and adolescent manatees have been known to join their mothers during migration. Sometimes, manatees come upon other manatees just by swimming in the same waters.

When two manatees are seen together, they are most often a mother and her young. A young manatee is called a calf. Sometimes, large numbers of manatees are seen together. The group is usually made up of a single female and several males trying to mate with her. A large number of manatees may also be seen gathering in warm water when cold weather cools the water temperature below 68° Fahrenheit (20° Celsius).

Scientists have observed some of these encounters. They have noted specific behaviors showing that, as solitary as these animals can be at times, they do enjoy being with other manatees. Manatees have been observed swimming together, diving together, and playing with each other. Scientists have also observed manatees hugging each other with their flippers and sharing a nap on the water's floor with their tails touching.

From an Expert

"Protecting manatees protects Florida's way of life. By protecting manatees and their **habitat**, we ensure clean water, lush sea grass beds, and pristine habitats. We have a responsibility to make sure our grandchildren's grandchildren will get a chance to enjoy the vast array of wildlife diversity we're lucky enough to see on a regular basis."
Suzanne Tarr

Suzanne Tarr was a staff biologist with the Save the Manatee Club. She is now a project leader for the manatee photo-identification program at the Florida Fish and Conservation Commission.

Keys to
Manatees

Manatees are far-sighted. This means they can see things far away better than things that are close.

After a manatee rubs its scent on rocks, other manatees can taste them to help navigate at night. Scent marking may be referred to as a sixth sense called smell-taste.

Communication

Manatees are intelligent and curious creatures. They demonstrate these traits through their love of play. Sometimes, a group of manatees will get together to play a game of tag or follow-the-leader. During these activities, the manatees can often be heard communicating with each other with various squeals and squeaks.

Most of the communication between manatees occurs between a mother and her calf. Mothers communicate with their young through high-pitched squeals. Other forms of manatee communication include **scent markings**.

Manatees seldom make sounds with other adults. Even during mating there is little **vocalization**. Manatees do, however, send out calls to one another from time to time. Calling may signal that a manatee wants another manatee to approach, or it may indicate that the manatee wants to approach the other animal. These messages are conveyed through changes in the pitch, loudness, duration, or harshness of the sounds. Such vocalization is limited, however. When feeding or moving from one location to another, a manatee will vocalize only about once every 10 minutes.

A female manatee, called a cow, and her calf are most vocal when they are approaching or moving away from each other. This communication might last only a few seconds or continue for several minutes. There appear to be two reasons for this behavior. It signals that the calf is approaching to nurse or that the mother senses danger.

Scent plays an important role in the life of manatees. The animals leave scent markings at various sites by rubbing against objects. In Florida's Crystal River, where manatees have been studied closely, several traditional rubbing sites are used year after year. Such rubbing sites are usually large logs or rocks. If a rubbing site, such as a sunken log, disappears, the manatees will find something else that is nearby to use. Females rub more than males do. The places on their bodies most often associated with rubbing are those where there are **glandular secretions**, including the area underneath their flippers and their chin.

Scientists think there are several reasons for this behavior. Rubbing may help to get rid of parasites that live on the manatee's skin. It may also serve to let males know when a female is ready to mate.

Body Language

Body language plays an important role in manatee communication. Manatees use their noses, tails, and bodies to share information. They have many ways of communicating with one another and with other animals.

Threat Displays

Manatees sometimes use their bodies to push away an unwanted intruder. Often, this happens when another manatee has come too close, but they have done the same thing to human divers who get too close to them. A mother will also position her body between an intruder and her calf.

Tail Slapping

Male manatees sometimes slap the surface of the water with their tails. They also lunge their bodies at each other. This is a signal of aggression during mating. A male using this body language is trying to keep other males away from the female it is trying to mate with.

Barrel-rolling

Florida manatees barrel-roll and swim upside down. They have also been spotted body-surfing together on fast water currents. These activities are a form of play for Florida manatees.

Touching Noses

When two manatees meet, they often touch noses. It is as if they are greeting with a "kiss." Nose touching may be a way for the two manatees to identify each other.

Should manatees be kept in zoos and aquariums?

Manatees live in zoos and aquariums around the world. At the South Florida Museum, more than one million people have visited the oldest manatee in captivity, Snooty, who turned 65 years old in 2013. Some people are against ocean mammals being kept in captivity.

FOR

1. Daily visitors of all ages are able to see Snooty and other manatees in captivity up close. Learning about these animals encourages visitors to support the protection of all species and their environments.
2. Many manatees in captivity today were rescued for various reasons from nature and brought back to health. They will be returned to their natural habitat if possible.

AGAINST

1. Manatees require more space to thrive than a zoo or aquarium can provide.
2. Manatee calves raised in zoos and aquariums do not learn how to survive in their natural habitat. Older manatees in captivity lose the learned behaviors that would help them survive in nature.

Keys to **Manatees**

The manatee is very resistant to diseases. It has a strong immune system that protects it from germs.

The manatee calf nurses from the milk sources located underneath its mother's front flippers.

Mating and Birth

When a female is ready to mate, she will attract a group of males. They will compete for her attention. This mating herd may stay together for several weeks. During this time, the males shove and push each other, trying to get close to the female. One male will dominate the mating for a while. When he becomes tired, he is replaced by another male, who will dominate the mating until he, too, gets tired and is replaced. It is not uncommon for a female to have six to eight males in a mating herd. There is at least one report of a female attracting 17 males.

Manatees do not have a specific breeding season. A female may be ready to mate at any time. However, mating and calving activity seems to peak in the spring and early summer.

Following mating, the female manatee often goes off on her own. She will seek peaceful places to rest and graze, or feed on grasses and plants. The **gestation period** for manatees is between 12 and 14 months. When she is ready to give birth, the female will try to find a quiet area where she will not be disturbed.

The birth takes place underwater, but the calf is quickly urged to the water's surface to take its first breath of air. As manatee calves grow older, their regular breathing rhythm will decrease from once every 20 seconds to once every 4 minutes or longer. Manatees normally take a breath every 3 to 5 minutes. This can slow to one breath every 10 to 20 minutes when they are resting.

A manatee calf can swim shortly after birth, usually within an hour. It does not stray from its mother, however, but swims alongside her. In this way, the manatee calf can nurse. A newborn calf quickly forms a strong bond with its mother. At first, the calf nurses for three to five minutes every one to two hours. This time increases as the calf grows and needs more milk.

Calves

Manatee mothers give birth about once every two to five years. Normally, only one calf is born at a time, but twins have been known to occur. The mother raises her young alone. Manatee males play no role in caring for calves.

After birth, over the next two to three years, the mother will guide the calf to adulthood. There is much for a young manatee to learn. The mother will introduce the calf to feeding areas and show the calf what it should eat. Manatees avoid eating plants such as spatterdock and water pennywort that have naturally occurring poisons called toxins. The mother will also show the calf where to find the warm waters so necessary to its survival. Though mothers and calves stay together for at least two years, a calf will nurse for only about the first year of its life.

The mother keeps a close eye on the calf and is always on the watch for danger. If she senses danger, she will quickly take action. She may sound a vocal alarm to call the calf to her side. Once the calf has come to her, both mother and calf will flee from the area.

The Florida manatee calf measures about 4.5 feet (1.4 m).

Manatees do not have eyelashes. They have eyelids that slide across the eyeball for protection.

If a Florida manatee gives birth to twin calves, she may nurse them at the same time.

Keys to
Manatees

The skin under a manatee's neck and flippers is loose and jiggles.

Most mammals have seven neck vertebrae, or small bones that form the backbone. The manatee has only six, which means it must turn its entire body to look behind it.

Development

At birth, a manatee looks very much like a smaller version of an adult manatee. However, its coloring is dark gray instead of brown or light gray. The skin color becomes lighter within the manatee's first month of life.

Newborn manatees weigh about 60 pounds (27 kg) and are about 4 feet (1.2 m) long. Calves begin to nurse within a few hours of birth. By the third or fourth month of life, the calf begins to eat some of the same types of underwater plants that its mother eats.

The first two years are a time of rapid growth for the manatee. In its first year alone, its weight can jump to approximately 700 pounds (315 kg), and it can add another 2 feet (0.6 m) to its length. The calf continues to nurse during this time. It needs frequent nourishment from its mother as it continues its rapid rate of growth.

After the calf's first year, the mother usually begins to stop feeding the young manatee her milk. By the end of the second year, she will have introduced the calf to all of the available food items in its habitat. She will also have shown the calf the migration routes she uses to move from place to place at different times of the year. The calf is then ready to leave its mother's side.

Not all calves leave their mothers at the 2-year mark. Even the calves that separate from their mothers often stay in nearby waters where they can maintain contact. When it is time to migrate, offspring that are no longer nursing are known to tag along with their mother on the journey to their summer or winter home.

By about 4 years of age, the female manatee is entering adulthood. She will be ready to mate sometime between her fourth and ninth years. A female will be able to bear young for about 20 years. Some studies suggest that males mature later than females do, reaching adulthood when they are 6 to 9 years of age.

Habitat

There would be no Florida manatees if it were not for the warm-water sources along the Florida coast. In winter, most Florida manatees can be found at these warm-water sources. They will venture into more northern waters in the summer months, when the water temperature is warmer.

Unlike most other sea mammals, Florida manatees live and travel in both fresh and salt water. Florida manatees normally stay close to shore. They can travel, rest, play, feed, and mate in shallow water that is only 3 to 10 feet (1 to 3 m) deep. Depending on the season, Florida manatees will rest from 2 to 12 hours a day. They remain motionless, either on the surface or on the bottom of the sea floor.

Organizing the Ocean

Earth is home to millions of different **organisms**, all of which have specific survival needs. These organisms rely on their environment, or the place where they live, for their survival. All plants and animals have relationships with their environment. They interact with the environment itself, as well as the other plants and animals within the environment. These interactions create **ecosystems**.

Ecosystems can be broken down into levels of organization. These levels range from a single plant or animal to many species of plants and animals living together in an area.

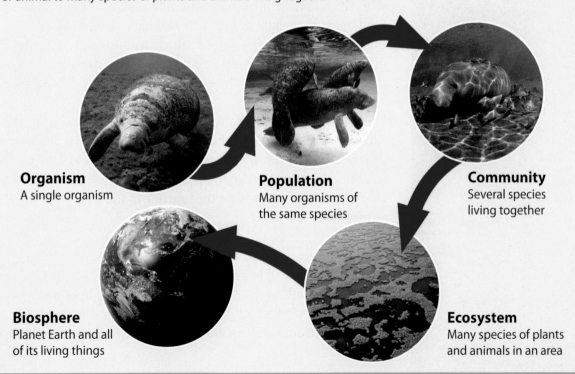

Organism
A single organism

Population
Many organisms of the same species

Community
Several species living together

Biosphere
Planet Earth and all of its living things

Ecosystem
Many species of plants and animals in an area

Manatees cannot tolerate water below 46°F (9°C).

Manatee sightings in Alabama, Georgia, and South Carolina waters are common during the summer months.

Animals on the Brink

Range

Florida manatees are found in the shallow waters along the southeastern coast of the United States. They also enter rivers and lagoons. A lagoon is a shallow body of water separated from the sea by sandbars or reefs. In winter, most manatees are found in Florida waters. In summer, they may migrate as far north as North Carolina and as far west as Texas.

Their range is defined by water temperature. Although they are warm-blooded animals, manatees cannot continue to maintain their body temperature in very cold water. Manatees in cold water will not survive long. They prefer waters with temperatures above 68°F (20°C). Hot summer weather allows them to expand their range as the waters along the coastline warm. The return of cold weather in fall forces the animals to retreat to areas where the water is consistently warm.

A manatee can travel an average of 40 to 50 miles (64 to 80 kilometers) a day. Some manatees, most often males, will travel even farther. One wandering male had to be rescued from the chilly waters of Chesapeake Bay, which is between Maryland and Virginia. The manatee was flown back to Florida.

Florida is an ideal place for manatees because it has many natural springs. At these springs, very warm water rises from beneath the ground into rivers, streams, and other bodies of fresh water. The springs make these waters warmer. As rivers and streams flow into the sea, coastal waters are warmed, as well. The average temperature of the water flowing from springs ranges from 70°F to 84°F (21°C to 29°C), warm enough to support the manatee. The Crystal River spring provides warm water to an important winter habitat for manatees.

As important as these springs are, manatees will also use human-made sources of warm water. Electric-power plants and factories along several of Florida's rivers use river water to cool down their machinery. This water becomes very warm by the time it is put back into the river. These plants have provided manatees with another set of warm-water refuges.

Warm water is only one of the manatee's habitat needs. Manatees also need plenty of aquatic plants. In addition, they must have access to fresh water. Like humans, manatees cannot drink salt water. Their bodies are poorly equipped to get rid of excess salt. Manatees must drink fresh water from time to time. The perfect mixture of saltwater and freshwater habitats can be found in bays, lagoons, and **estuaries**. These bodies of water are fed with a constant source of fresh water from a river or stream.

Keys to **Manatees**

Manatees can replace 90 percent of the stale air in their lungs with fresh air in one breath. That compares with only 10 to 15 percent for humans.

In the cold months, groups of manatees find warm water near various power plants in Florida waters. Each year, they return to about 20 major sites.

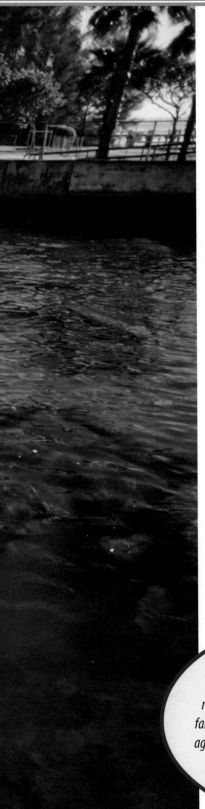

Migration

For the Florida manatee, the year can be divided into two seasons. During the warmer months, manatees migrate to favorite feeding grounds along the southeastern coast. Manatee migration does not occur in large herds. Individual manatees migrate with other individuals in small groups. It is likely that manatees follow the same routes that they traveled with their mothers.

Cold weather forces manatees to return to places near the Florida coast where they can almost always find warm water. These areas have natural springs and human-made sources of warm water. Manatees spend the winter in various regular sites in Florida.

When manatees migrate from their summer feeding areas to wintering areas, they usually follow the shoreline and avoid the deep, open ocean. They use deeper channels to get to the shallow waters where they feed and rest. The movement of manatees between wintering areas and summer areas allows the vegetation in each area to replenish itself in the months that manatees are not feeding there. This ensures that the manatees have a year-round supply of food.

From an Expert

"It was thought that sufficient protection for manatees could be achieved by implementing local management plans. If, however, manatees are moving farther north into Georgia and the Carolinas, governmental agencies, private industry, and conservation organizations will have to reassess their strategies for protecting manatees and their habitat."
Galen Rathbun

Galen Rathbun is a research biologist. For many years, he served as project leader for the U.S. Fish and Wildlife Service's programs for the Florida manatee and other animals.

Diet

Sirenians are the only mammals in the world to feed almost entirely on ocean and freshwater vegetation. They are **herbivores**. Manatees eat a wide variety of mostly aquatic plants.

The manatee's preferred plants include sea grass, water hyacinth, and hydrilla. These plants flourish in warm **subtropical** waters. Manatees may take in other animals, such as sea squirts and mollusks, that cling to the grass they are eating.

Manatees sometimes feed on land plants that hang over the water.

The amount of food manatees eat each day is often between 8 percent and 20 percent of their body weight. The minimum daily amount of plant material a manatee must eat is between 4 to 8 percent of its weight. That means, for example, that an 800-pound (360-kg) manatee needs to eat at least 32 pounds (15 kg) of vegetation a day.

Much of the food that a manatee eats is low in nutritional value. Manatees must spend five to eight hours a day feeding to get the energy and nutrients they need to survive. Sometimes they grasp the food with their flippers to hold it as they graze. To digest food with such low nutritional value, manatees have an extra-large stomach and very long intestines. The increased size of their digestive system allows them to extract the most nutrients available from their food.

A manatee's intestines are 150 feet (45 m) long. Between the large and small intestine is an area where bacteria break down much of the plant material called cellulose. Manatees can break down cellulose better than almost any other living mammal.

The large body of the manatee also aids in the digestion of food. Digested food energy that the manatee does not need to use right away is stored in blubber beneath its skin and around its intestines. This blubber helps protect the digestive process from the effects of cooler water that would slow down the process.

Blubber is also important to the manatee in another way. Food energy stored there can be used by the manatee to survive if it goes through a long period when little or no food is available. This is most likely to happen in winter, when there is much less new plant growth than at other times of the year.

Keys to
Manatees

Manatees are known to eat 10 species of algae and a total of 44 other species of plants.

When a manatee has something to eat, it wraps its prehensile lip around the food and works it into the mouth.

The Food Cycle

A food cycle shows how energy in the form of food is passed from one living thing to another. As Florida manatees feed and move through the water, they affect the lives of other living things. In the diagram below, the arrows show the flow of energy from one living thing to another through a **food web**.

Primary Consumers
Manatees feed on sea grasses and other plants that thrive in the subtropical waters of Florida.

Secondary Consumers
Both alligators and crocodiles share the manatee's habitat. They seldom attack a healthy manatee, but they will feed on a dead one.

Parasites
Florida manatees provide a home for parasites such as wormlike creatures called helminths and fungi called microsporidia. The skin of a manatee also provides a good place for algae to grow.

Producers

Tiny plants called **plankton**, sea grasses, and other plants live in fresh and salt water. They use sunlight to produce food energy.

Decomposers

When a manatee dies, decomposers break down its body materials. This adds nutrients to the water that help plankton and other aquatic plants to thrive.

CAUTION

MANATEE AREA

Take a Stand
Debate • Research

Should Florida manatees remain a protected species?

U.S. and Florida laws protect manatees from hunters. In some areas, boating is limited. Some people feel enough manatees swim in Florida waters. Others believe manatees still need protection.

FOR

1. Manatee cows have very few young compared to many other types of animals. If large numbers of manatees die as a result of human activity, the manatee population may not be able to recover.
2. Manatees are not aggressive animals, and they have few means of defending themselves. Giving them protected status helps keep people away from the animals, reducing the risk that they will be harmed.

AGAINST

1. If the number of manatees becomes too large, they will put at risk other **threatened** and **endangered** species, including sea grass.
2. Manatee populations are becoming a nuisance in some areas, especially around power plants, where they are now gathering in high numbers. A population boom affects the entire ecosystem by destroying plants native to the area and by reducing the food available to other animals.

It is not unusual to see a manatee with scars from collisions with motorboat propellers in the waters of Florida.

Competition

Florida manatees have no real **predators** in nature. They live peacefully with other marine animals. Manatees sometimes face competition from their environment. Harsh conditions, such as cold weather, can kill them in large numbers. Florida Fish and Wildlife Conservation Commission officials blamed the unusual cold for a high number of deaths in 2010. Almost 280 manatee deaths that year were tied to low water temperatures.

An occurrence called red tide can also harm manatee populations. A red tide is caused by a bloom of natural algae that stains the water a reddish-brown color. The algae carry a toxin that attacks the nervous systems of any animals that come into contact with it. The animals die because they cannot breathe. Red tides are also called harmful algal blooms.

A harmful algal bloom occurs nearly every summer along Florida's Gulf Coast. In the first five months of 1996, for example, about 150 manatees died. This was more than 5 percent of Florida's total manatee population at the time. In 2013, a harmful algal bloom in Florida caused at least 276 manatee deaths. Deaths from the same cause in the previous year numbered 33.

Humans are by far the Florida manatee's greatest competition. This competition comes in the form of both human activity and human progress. Many manatee deaths occur each year when the animals are hit by boats. Manatees also fall victim to the development of waterway systems. Florida is a popular tourist destination. As more and more people arrive to visit and to live, changes to the environment occur. These changes sometimes hurt the manatee and its habitat.

Harmful algal blooms have killed several types of animals, including loggerhead turtles, in Florida.

Keys to **Manatees**

In Portuguese, the term for manatee is *peixe-boi*, or "fish cow." In Spanish, it is *vaca marina*, or "sea cow."

The calm, slow-moving Florida manatee allows small fish to feed on the algae that grow on its body.

Florida Manatees with Other Animals

Florida manatees share the water with many other sea creatures, including various fish and turtle species, river otters, alligators, and crocodiles. Manatees tend to avoid confrontations with their neighbors. If threatened by another animal, a manatee will flee instead of standing its ground.

Even the alligator tends to leave the manatee alone. This is probably because of the manatee's massive size. Its size, tough hide, and preference for near-shore waters help it avoid many ocean predators large enough to be a threat.

Historically, humans hunted manatees for their blubber and their meat. Today, the greatest threat to the Florida manatee's survival is boaters. In recent years, collisions with motorboats have accounted for more than one-fourth of manatee deaths in Florida.

In many states, manatees face habitat loss. More development and an increased human population affect manatee habitats and food sources. Floodgates now control the flow of water in many rivers and streams. Sewage treatment plants have been built near coastal waters. Manatees sometimes get caught in the machinery of these flood-control and sewage systems. They can be crushed or drowned as a result. The opening and closing of floodgates has been known to separate a calf from its mother, resulting in almost certain death for the calf. As the human population grows, water pollution and landfill projects are also increasing. These, too, contribute to the loss of habitat and food for the manatee.

"Boat-manatee collisions are a problem. They are a major part of overall manatee mortality. They are also the problem that we are more likely able to do something about."
James Powell

James Powell is the executive director and cofounder of Sea to Shore Alliance. He was a director of National and Aquatic Programs at the Wildlife Trust. He also coordinated the marine mammal and sea turtle program at the Florida Fish and Wildlife Conservation Commission's Florida Wildlife Research Institute.

Folklore

In 1493, navigator for Spain Christopher Columbus explored the area now known as the Caribbean. His crew saw creatures rise out of the water and splash their tails. They thought the creatures were mermaids, with the head and upper body of a woman and the tail of a fish. Most people now believe they were manatees.

Manatees share a long history with the native groups of the Caribbean. In most cases, the manatee was a food source for these people. As a result, their folklore centers around hunting and food preparation rituals.

The Rama people of coastal Nicaragua believe that it is important to return the bones of a manatee to where it was killed. A successful hunter is also given the manatee's earbones because the Rama believe manatees cannot hear the approach of someone wearing manatee earbones. Manatee earbones are used as charms to ward off witchcraft in the Yucatan Peninsula of Mexico. In Guatemala, these bones are thought to ease the pain of childbirth.

Throughout history, the manatee's presence has generated many stories. Early native groups believed they shared common bonds with the manatee. In South America, the Warauno people, as well as other native groups in Brazil, believe that the manatee has human beginnings.

A modern folktale has developed along the Atlantic coast of the United States. In 1994, a male manatee was sighted in Chesapeake Bay, hundreds of miles (km) north of its typical range. The manatee, called Chessie, was a big celebrity until the weather turned cold. Fearing for his health, scientists captured Chessie and flew him back to Florida's warmer waters. The next year, Chessie made the 500-mile (800-km) journey to Chesapeake Bay again. In fact, he went farther, going as far north as Rhode Island before turning back to Florida. Chessie was last seen in 2011.

Manatees are sometimes the subject of sculptures in Florida.

Myth	VS	Fact
 Manatees always move very slowly.		Manatees normally travel between 3 and 5 miles (5 and 8 km) per hour. They can travel up to 20 miles (32 km) per hour in short bursts if necessary.
 Manatees are clumsy creatures.		Its shape helps a manatee move gracefully through the water. Manatees can often be seen performing somersaults and other acrobatic activities.
 Manatees were brought to Florida in the mid-1900s to control the growth of water hyacinth.		Fossil remains indicate that manatees have lived in the Florida area for about 45 million years. Water hyacinth is a nuisance plant in Florida, but manatees do very little to control its growth. While manatees feed on the plant, they are not able to eat it as quickly as it grows.

Rock paintings in Western Australia show dugongs. Like manatees, dugongs belong to the order of animals called Sirenians.

Status

The Florida Fish and Wildlife Conservation Commission was not able to conduct an annual survey of the state's manatees in 2012 or 2103 because the weather was warmer than average. The last recorded survey of Florida manatees took place at the beginning of 2011. At that time, 4,834 animals were counted. That was up from about 3,300 in 2001. Scientists believe that manatee numbers have increased in some areas because the animal was given legal protection. Many scientists are concerned, however, that this population growth may not continue.

The U.S. Marine Mammal Protection Act has protected manatees in Florida waters since 1972. This act bans the hunting, harming, or harassment of manatees. It also forbids trade in manatee parts. Manatees are also protected under the Endangered Species Act of 1973. Under this act, the manatee was declared an endangered species in the United States. The manatee received additional legal protection in 1978 under the Florida Manatee Sanctuary Act. This act allowed Florida to establish sanctuaries, or protected areas, for manatees where boating is not permitted.

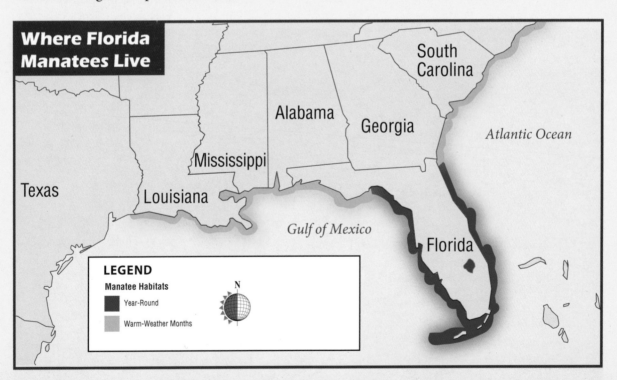

Where Florida Manatees Live

South Carolina

Alabama

Georgia

Atlantic Ocean

Mississippi

Texas

Louisiana

Gulf of Mexico

Florida

LEGEND
Manatee Habitats
- Year-Round
- Warm-Weather Months

N

To help put an end to Florida manatee deaths in accidents, the U.S. Fish and Wildlife Service (FWS) has developed a manatee recovery plan. As a result, boat regulations are in place where manatees are common. "Go slow" warnings have been posted on rivers frequented by manatees. In some areas, boats are banned.

The FWS has also developed sanctuaries where manatees are able to live in relative peace. People who threaten or harm manatees can be fined. Construction companies operating in waters where manatees are known to travel must post signs warning workers that manatees are found there. If a manatee enters the area, it may be necessary to halt work until it leaves. Scientists are constantly reviewing the situation with an eye toward helping the manatee.

The manatee has benefited from the FWS plan and other efforts. Local citizens and tourists have helped by reporting injured or dead manatees. This has helped scientists link human activities to manatee deaths.

Many problems remain. Manatees are still killed in boat collisions. Other threats include getting entangled in fishing nets and swallowing fishing lures. Manatees continue to be crushed and drowned in flood-control structures. A growing human population is putting more and more demands on Florida's water resources, threatening natural springs. Aging power plants, so important for the warm water they provide, may have to be rebuilt. This may deprive Florida manatees of the warm waters they need in the winter.

Take a Stand
· Debate ·
· Research ·

Should motorboats in Florida be required to have propeller guards in order to protect manatees?

Powerboats kill many manatees each year. Most of these manatees die from hull impact. However, some die after being injured by the blades of a boat propeller. Manufacturers have developed guards to cover the blades. These guards can help reduce manatee injuries and deaths.

FOR

1. Protecting the Florida manatee is the only way to maintain the population and promote its growth. Any measures that help protect an endangered species from injury or death should be taken.
2. The Florida manatee is an important part of the natural beauty of the state. Without all of Florida's unique wildlife, its tourism industry would suffer.

AGAINST

1. Some people think using propeller guards is a substitute for following slow-speed rules. If boaters using the guards do not obey speed limits, more accidents that harm manatees may occur.
2. Passing these kinds of regulations may hurt Florida's recreation and tourism industry. Businesses and people in the state will lose money as a result.

Saving the Florida Manatee

The U.S. Geological Survey's Sirenia Project is based in Gainesville, Florida. The program was established in 1974 to study the Florida manatee. Its scientists are dedicated to helping the manatee survive in the modern world.

The scientists in the Sirenia Project have photographed and cataloged manatees. They pay close attention to the scars that mark Florida manatees. Researchers developed an image-based computer program to identify permanently marked manatees. Most manatees have had encounters with boat propellers. The scar patterns from these accidents are as individual as human fingerprints.

This collected information is now part of a national database. It helps scientists to track specific manatees and to create a history of their lives. Each time that a scientist identifies a manatee, information on its location, activities, and possible companions becomes part of the database. Over time, this information creates a profile of individual manatees.

Groups often work together to rescue and nurse injured or sick manatees back to health. In 2009, a manatee nicknamed Patsy was released after biologists at the Florida Fish and Wildlife Conservation Commission and other volunteers rescued her. The manatee's flipper had become entangled in fishing line.

More than 2,000 manatees living in Florida waters have been entered in the Sirenia Project database. The database helps scientists learn more about manatee behavior, migration, and groups. Scientists have also used the database to study the effect on manatees of a large 2010 oil spill in the Gulf of Mexico. No manatee deaths have been found to be caused by this disaster, which was the worst oil spill in U.S. history.

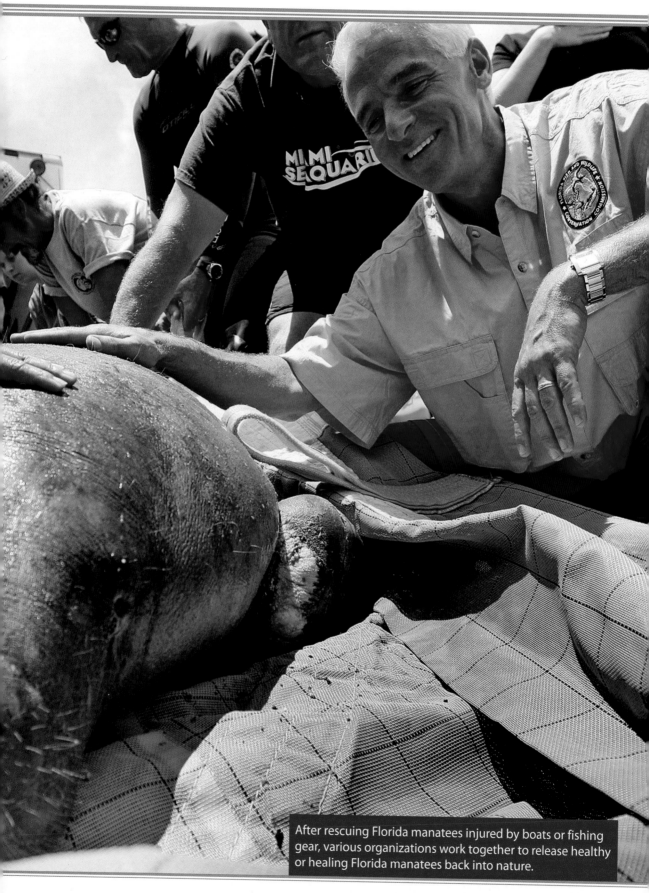

After rescuing Florida manatees injured by boats or fishing gear, various organizations work together to release healthy or healing Florida manatees back into nature.

Back from the Brink

Tracking manatees has become easier with advanced radio and satellite devices. When tracking a manatee, scientists put a small, portable unit onto a belt that is attached to the manatee's body. The unit sends out a particular series of beeps that allows scientists to identify the manatee. If tracking by radio, scientists follow the signal from a boat or plane. Satellite tracking uses a similar system, but its receivers are mounted on satellites circling Earth. The satellites then send information to scientists' computers.

These two systems make it possible to track the movements of manatees around the clock. They allow researchers to identify key manatee areas. The tracking information is also useful for making recommendations to protect manatees.

There are many ways to help protect the Florida manatee. You could:

- Support related conservation groups.
- Write a letter to your local newspaper to educate your community about manatees.
- Observe all posted signs when you are on the water.
- Share details about any manatee sightings and report any injured manatees.

Florida manatees are fascinating animals that need people's help. For more information about manatees and how to protect them, contact:

**Southeast Ecological Science Center/
Sirenia Project**
7920 NW 71st Street
Gainesville, FL 32653

Save the Manatee Club
500 N. Maitland Avenue
Maitland, FL 32751

One reason it is illegal to feed, touch, or provide fresh water to a manatee is that these actions may encourage the animal to approach people and place it in harm's way.

Activity

Debating helps people think about ideas thoughtfully and carefully. When people debate, two sides take a different viewpoint on a subject. Each side takes turns presenting arguments to support its view.

Use the Take a Stand sections found throughout this book as a starting point for debate topics. Organize your friends or classmates into two teams. One team will argue in favor of the topic, and the other will argue against. Each team should research the issue thoroughly using reliable sources of information, including books, scientific journals, and trustworthy websites. Take notes of important facts that support your side of the debate. Prepare your argument using these facts to support your opinion.

During the debate, the members of each team are given a set amount of time to make their arguments. The team arguing the For side goes first. They have five minutes to present their case. All members of the team should participate equally. Then, the team arguing the Against side presents its arguments. Each team should take notes of the main points the other team argues.

After both teams have made their arguments, they get three minutes to prepare their rebuttals. Teams review their notes from the previous round. The teams focus on trying to disprove each of the main points made by the other team using solid facts. Each team gets three minutes to make its rebuttal. The team arguing the Against side goes first. Students and teachers watching the debate serve as judges. They should try to judge the debate fairly using a standard score sheet, such as the example below.

Criteria	Rate: 1-10	Sample Comments
1. Were the arguments well organized?	8	logical arguments, easy to follow
2. Did team members participate equally?	9	divided time evenly between members
3. Did team members speak loudly and clearly?	3	some members were difficult to hear
4. Were rebuttals specific to the other team's arguments?	6	rebuttals were specific, more facts needed
5. Was respect shown for the other team?	10	all members showed respect to the other team

2. What small, gopher-sized animal does the manatee share a common ancestor with?

3. How often do manatees normally take a breath?

1. How many subspecies of West Indian manatees are there?

5. How long is the gestation period for manatees?

6. Why might manatees touch noses?

4. How much does the average Florida manatee calf weigh at birth?

8. How is a manatee different from most other sea mammals?

9. At what age does the female manatee enter adulthood?

7. Why are manatees called herbivores?

10. How many Florida manatees are there?

Answers:
1. two 2. the hyrax 3. every 3 to 5 minutes 4. about 60 pounds (27 kg) 5. between 12 and 14 months 6. It may be a way to identify each other. 7. because they eat only plants 8. It lives and travels in both fresh and salt water. 9. about 4 years of age 10. According to a 2011 survey, there are 4,834.

Key Words

algae: rootless green, red or brown organisms that grow mostly in water

aquatic: living in or near the water

buoyancy: the ability to float in fluid

density: the amount of something in a certain space

ecosystems: communities of living things and resources

endangered: a type of plant or animal that exists in such small numbers that it is in danger of no longer surviving in the world or in a certain area

estuaries: lower ends of a river where the currents meet the ocean tides

food web: connecting food chains that show how energy flows from one organism to another through diet

gestation period: the length of time that a female is pregnant

glandular secretions: substances that ooze from a body organ

habitat: the place where an animal lives, grows, and raises its young

herbivores: animals that feed only on plants

mammals: warm-blooded animals that have hair or fur and nurse their young

mammary glands: body parts that produce milk

order: one of eight major ranks used to classify animals, between class and family

organisms: forms of life

plankton: floating and drifting tiny organisms in the sea

predators: animals that live by hunting other animals for food

prehensile: specially adapted for gripping objects

scent markings: odors an animal leaves behind, by droppings, urine, or rubbing against an object, that let other animals know it has been in an area

species: groups of individuals with common characteristics

subtropical: relating to the regions bordering on the Tropics, which is the part of Earth near the equator where the climate is warmest

threatened: at risk of becoming endangered

vocalization: sound made to send messages or to express emotions

Index

Log on to www.av2books.com

AV² by Weigl brings you media enhanced books that support active learning. Go to www.av2books.com, and enter the special code found on page 2 of this book. You will gain access to enriched and enhanced content that supplements and complements this book. Content includes video, audio, weblinks, quizzes, a slide show, and activities.

AV² Online Navigation

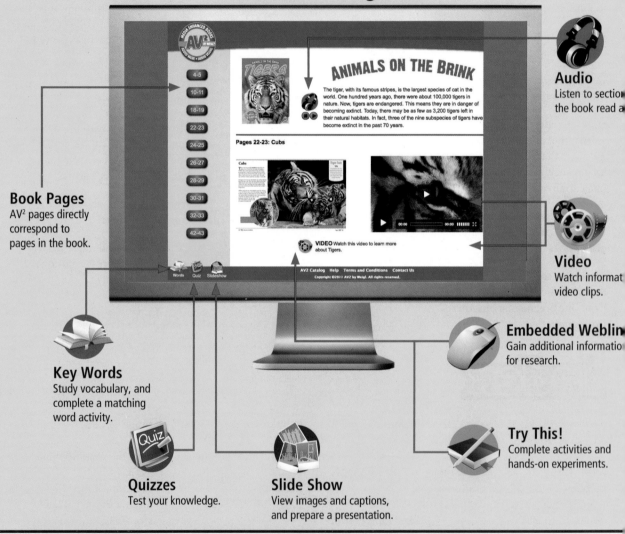

Book Pages
AV² pages directly correspond to pages in the book.

Key Words
Study vocabulary, and complete a matching word activity.

Quizzes
Test your knowledge.

Slide Show
View images and captions, and prepare a presentation.

Audio
Listen to section the book read a

Video
Watch informat video clips.

Embedded Weblin
Gain additional informatio for research.

Try This!
Complete activities and hands-on experiments.

AV² was built to bridge the gap between print and digital. We encourage you to tell us what you like and what you want to see in the future.

Sign up to be an AV² Ambassador at www.av2books.com/ambassador.

Due to the dynamic nature of the Internet, some of the URLs and activities provided as part of AV² by Weigl may have changed or ceased to exist. AV² by Weigl accepts no responsibility for any such changes. All media enhanced books are regularly monitored to update addresses and sites in a timely manner. Contact AV² by Weigl at 1-866-649-3445 or av2books@weigl.com with any questions, comments, or feedback.